S.Y.M.P.A.T.H.Y.

Sympathy: A Poem of Solace

ACRONYM POETRY GIFT SERIES

Copyright © 2021 by Macarena Luz Bianchi
MacarenaLuzB.com

Subscribe to the email list for this book spark.fyi/apc-s

Zonia Iqbal, Illustrator neon.ly/Zonial

Imprint

Spark Social, Inc.
Miami, FL USA
SparkSocialPress.com

ISBN: Hardcover: 978-1-954489-20-2
Paperback: 978-1-954489-21-9
Ebook: 978-1-954489-22-6

Ordering Information: Special discounts are available on quantity purchases by corporations, associations, and others. For details, contact the publisher.

S.I.M.P.A.T.H.Y.

A Poem of Solace

ACRONYM POETRY GIFT SERIES

Macarena Luz Bianchi

Imprint
Spark Social Press

Sorry for your loss.
My deepest condolences.

You are free to cry
and feel your sorrow.

Moment to moment,
acknowledge what you feel
with patience and grace.

Permission is yours to grieve
in any and every way.

Allow your feelings to flow
as you honor your loss.

Take your time and give yourself
the needed solace and space.

Haven of hugs will console you.
May you feel comfort's embrace.

Yours in sympathy, please be well.
You can cry, feel, and grieve freely,
for we know you are strong
and will carry on.

S.Y.M.P.A.T.H.Y.

A POEM OF SOLACE

Sorry for your loss. My deepest condolences.

You are free to cry and feel your sorrow.

Moment to moment, acknowledge what you feel with patience and grace.

Permission is yours to grieve in any and every way.

Allow your feelings to flow as you honor your loss.

Take your time and give yourself the needed solace and space.

Haven of hugs will console you. May you feel comfort's embrace.

Yours in sympathy, please be well. You can cry, feel, and grieve freely, for we know you are strong and will carry on.

Gift Book Series

ACRONYM POETRY COLLECTION

- *Congratulations: A Poem of Triumph*
- *Friendship: A Poem of Appreciation*
- *Intimacy: A Poem of Adoration*
- *Anniversary: A Poem of Affection*
- *Birthday: A Poem of Celebration.*
- *Valentine: A Poem of Love*

With more to come including: *Encouragement, Graduation*, and so on.

POETRY COLLECTION

- *Glorious Mom: A Poem of Appreciation*
- *Gratitude Is: A Lighthearted Empowerment Poem*
- *Gratitude Is: Poem & Coloring Book*
- *The Grateful Giraffes: What is Gratitude?*

About the Author

Macarena Luz Bianchi has a lighthearted and empowering approach and is affectionally considered a Fairy Godmother by her readers. She writes fiction and non-fiction for adults and children. She loves tea, flowers, and travel. Sign up for her newsletter and check out her other poems of appreciation, books, and more at MacarenaLuzB.com and subscribe to the email list for this book at spark.fyi/apc-s.

Lightning Source UK Ltd.
Milton Keynes UK
UKHW051502200821
389156UK00002B/44